demystifying

DIGITAL

photography

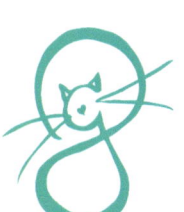

by demigail **napora**

DEMIGAIL PUBLISHING
BROADWAY, VA   22815

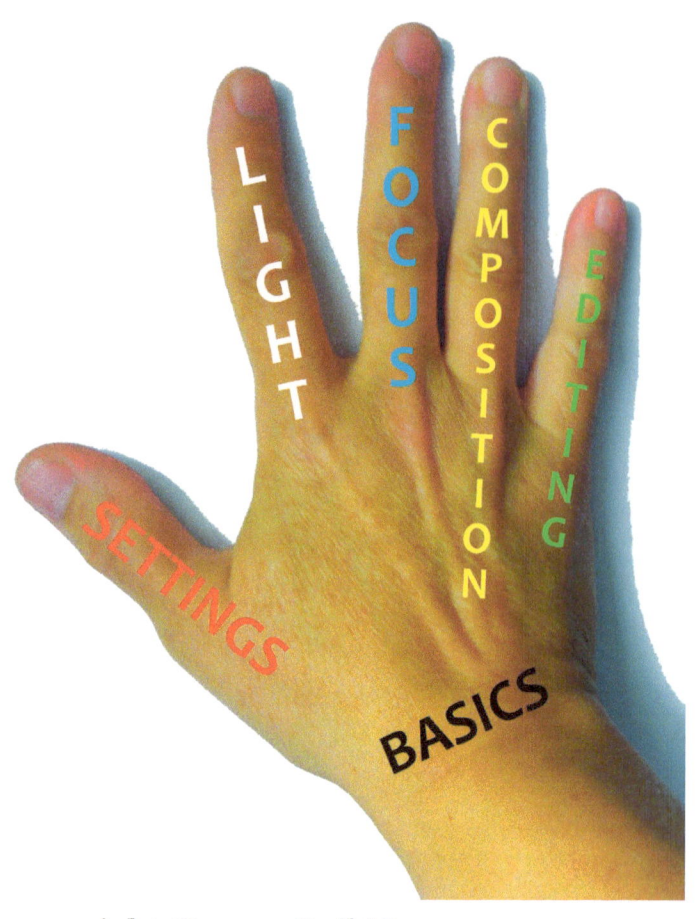

Text copyright ©2010 Gail Napora
Photos/Illustrations copyright ©2010 Gail Napora

For more information, visit www.demigail.com.

ISBN 145375489X
EAN 9781453754894

digital photography

has only been affordable for a short while. More computing power exists in a palm-sized camera now than was in my first home computer. This means that everyday people who have not been formally trained in taking pictures have an **80%**

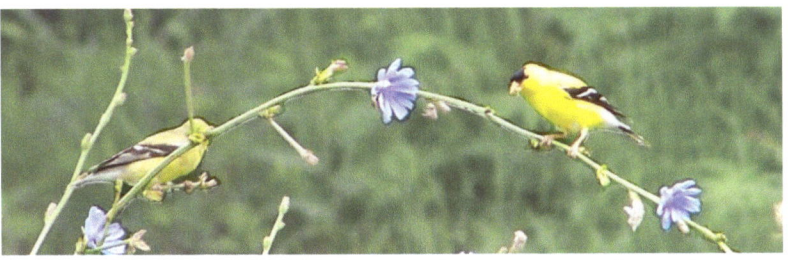

likelihood of getting a really good picture just by using the AUTO setting on the camera. If that 80% is NOT good enough for you, or you spend time wondering what went wrong because the picture you got doesn't match what you thought you captured, then this is the book for you. Once we cover the BASICS in this introduction, we will address the "five digits" of digital.

SETTINGS = are the mechanics of the machine; knowing what YOUR camera does (and doesn't) do

LIGHT = is the language of images (when the light is right, shoot)

FOCUS = refers to center and clarity (you can fix everything except focus)

COMPOSITION = is about design and style of your FRAME (PHI works every single time)

EDITING = is about improving excellence (make the best even better or elevate your image to 'art')

demystifying digital photography

is a practical way of understanding and using YOUR digital camera to consistently capture IMPRESSIVE images for personal and artistic use.

I present information in a format suited to the "everyday" picture taker, but with guidance and hints professionals can use to CONSISTENTLY produce better pictures.

demigail is my working name. I am a writer, artist and photographer who loves to help people succeed with their camera. I teach adults and youth in the community, at a local college, and individually, and I compiled this book based on those classes and the comments of the people I've taught.

Knowing each of us can learn anything, regardless of our age or ability, leads me to present information in a useful way. My genuine respect for the learner, and a belief that

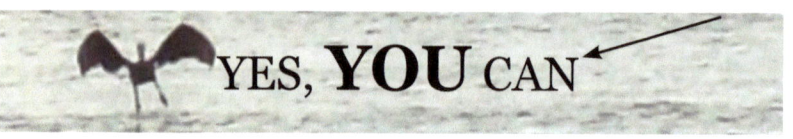
YES, **YOU** CAN

let's me provide ongoing encouragement while the learner travels from novice to expert. One of my favorite learners is a 91 year old aunt, who switched from a "disposable" to a digital camera when I visited for three days. Clearly she is the superstar, but she credits me with making it easy. I reviewed the following BASIC concepts with her, and know they will immediately help you get consistently better results from your camera.

1. **The camera is only a 'tool' for capturing your unique view of something. Thirty cameras 'focused' on a flower will have thirty similar but different images. HOW YOU choose to organize the frame, how you tilt or shift the lens to accept light, and the** clarity of the fore and background of the shot ALL speak to how you SEE it.

2. Anyone can master a 'tool' with repetition of use and evaluation of results. But every tool has its own basis for working, and the digital camera is no different. I believe that understanding that basis, the five digits of DEMYSTIFYING, allows a photographer to more quickly and efficiently evaluate and enhance their technique to achieve consistently better photographs.

3. Light is the language of the camera. In fact, the word photography means 'light writing' in Greek. Everything WE see is the reflection of light off an object. How our brain then presents the image to us is a result of our own editor: for example, fluorescent light is actually green, but our brain "translates" it to a more acceptable white/yellow light. In a digital camera, the AUTO setting will correct for fluorescent green 80% of the time. In a school, however, where there are dozens of fluorescent lights, the image will be green on AUTO: I see this in school yearbook candid shots all the time. We can change the setting in the camera, or edit it later, but the digital camera RECORDS THE REFLECTION OF LIGHT LITERALLY so things our brain would exclude are recorded.

4. In keeping with the previous point, I remind my learners that we have many editors, filters, and crops built into our brains from years of use. For example, when I am outside with a friend, I will SEE a butterfly immediately. My brain is practiced at noticing them. Your brain might have other preferences, and as such, you edit out things that don't match what you want to see, but the digital camera SEES EVERYTHING and RECORDS IT LITERALLY. When the resulting image is displayed, there are 'extra' things in the picture that we didn't notice, and don't want.

5. A camera 'sees' light in **3** colors: red, green, and blue (RGB). When we record light, or display it on a computer monitor (or TV) RGB is the basis from which we split it into millions of colors. An image recorded on your digital camera uses a PROGRAM to interpret reflected light and record it as tiny squares of color (PIXELS). Each camera has its own IMAGE SENSOR and PROGRAM, as well as a particular way of presenting color. Choose the brand that has color you like.

When we PRINT images, we use cyan-blue, magenta-red, yellow, and black (CMYK) to recreate the picture for paper. What we see on the well lit computer is rarely going to look like what we see from a printer, especially since different printers TRANSLATE colors differently.

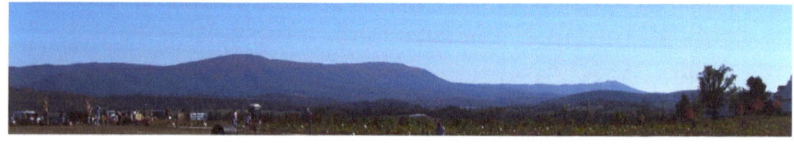

These BASIC concepts are the foundation of what follows: SETTINGS, LIGHT, FOCUS, COMPOSITION, **and** EDITING.

SETTINGS
beyond AUTO

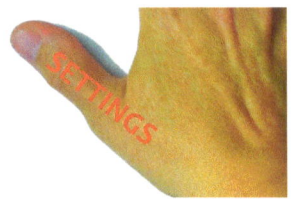

on a digital camera directly influence what is recorded on the image sensor. In class, each person comes with their camera and user manual, so you might benefit from having both handy as you read this section.

Everything you need to know **is** in your camera's user manual or its online equivalent. Unfortunately, these documents are not meant to 'teach' you. They are like a dictionary -- you have to know what you are looking for or the camera manual/internet search is useless.

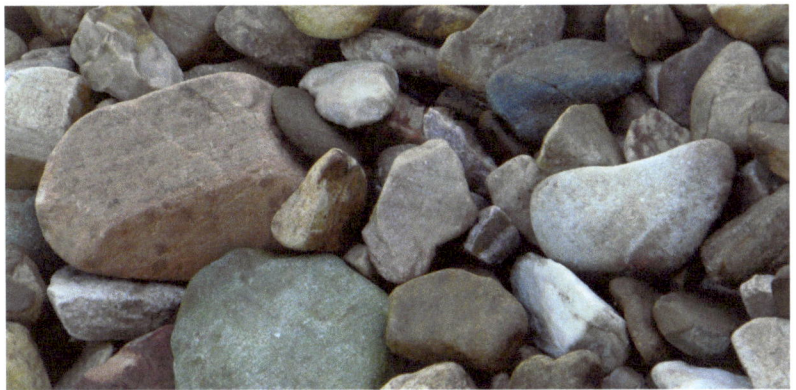

The most important 'button' on your camera is the **MENU** button. With it, almost everything you want to change or do is possible. Press menu, then use the 'compass' (circle with four arrows and an OK button in the middle) to find things. It is so simple that it is confusing.

My 91 year old aunt, 'got it' when I said it is just like a TV remote. To go up, you press the top of the circle; down on the bottom, right to right, and left to left. This is how you move; to ACT or 'enter' your choice, push the middle OK.

BEFORE YOU TURN YOUR CAMERA ON
- Make sure your lens is clean (using only a lens cloth);
- Check that the battery is charged according to directions (being cautious to avoid power surges);
- Be certain you haven't drastically changed temperature (going from cold to hot, indoors to out, or the reverse).

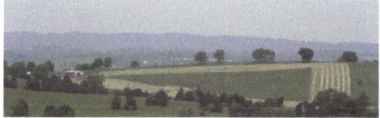 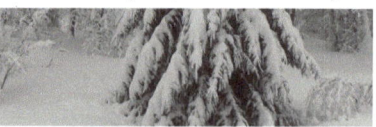

HOLD YOUR CAMERA WITH TWO HANDS, strap around your neck or wrist, elbows tucked tight to your sides and slowly press the button halfway to AUTOFOCUS, then the rest of the way to take a picture. This posture and technique, on AUTO setting, will yield great pictures with correct lighting and focus most of the time. Look at every single thing in the viewfinder or on the LCD screen when you COMPOSE or frame your picture and you can get a prize winning shot.

- Without your strap on you can drop the camera (if dropped while ON, you can destroy it; if OFF, not so bad).

- If you don't tuck the elbows, or press slowly, the camera will move during the IMAGE RECORDING process and pixels will shift causing the picture to seem out of focus. Most new digital cameras have IMAGE STABILIZATION which can help, but may not correct for everything.

- If you don't let the camera finish its AUTOFOCUS step, your image will NOT be in focus. The camera needs time to calculate LIGHT, APERTURE, **and** SHUTTER SPEED so you don't have to set them manually.

Now take lots of pictures before you go on reading ! ! ! You will have plenty of good, and many great shots, just by doing these few things I have suggested.

The factory settings are fine for most of us. Change or try different settings, but if you get lost, simply find the **RESET TO DEFAULT** choice on the menu and use it. My dear aunt accidentally chose Spanish as her language. She doesn't speak it, so the saving step was to RESET.

Camera settings affect either the **FORMAT** of the image, or the **RECORDING** of one specific image.

Think of FORMAT as the operating system where date, time, file size, and other things that apply to *ALL* pictures can be set.

RECORDING is where SCENE SETTINGS come in. Think of LIGHT, APERTURE, and SHUTTER SPEED, and the things that affect them, as you RECORD a single image or picture.

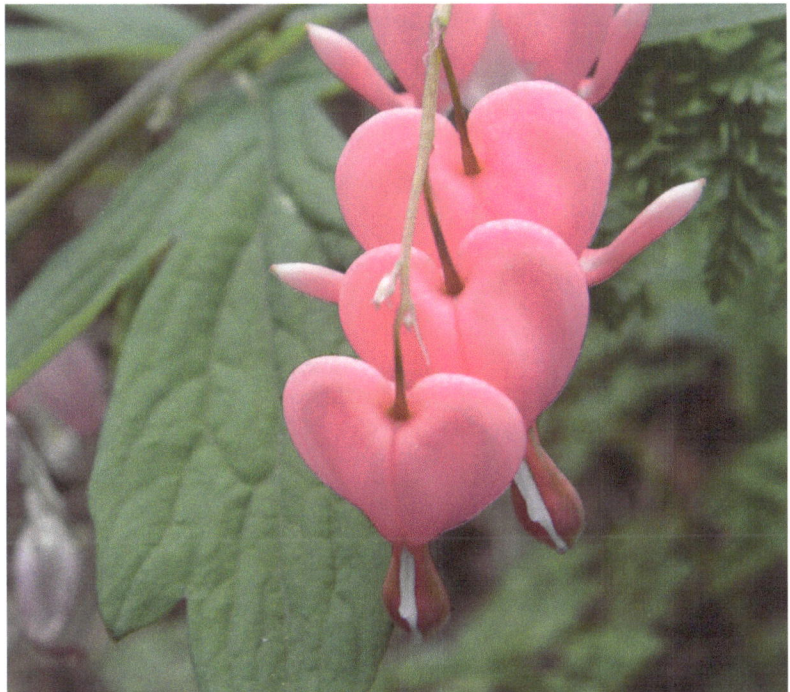

We'll cover some FORMAT settings first.

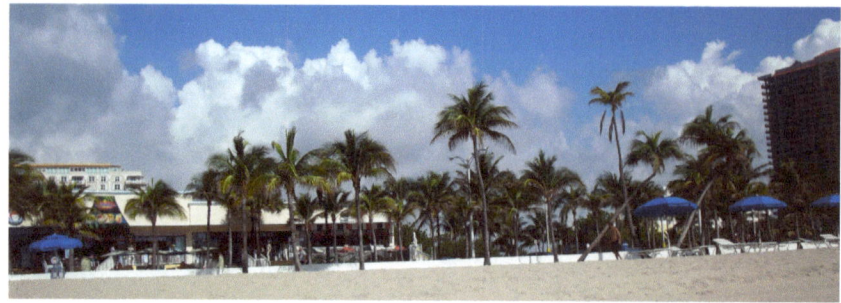

• **IMAGE STORAGE** decides where images are kept; if you have an SD (storage device) card, you can choose between it (hundreds of pictures) and internal memory (usually only 15-20 pictures). BE CAREFUL: if you choose to FORMAT an SD card that has already been used, it will erase whatever pictures you have on the card.

• **COMPRESSION OR FILE FORMAT** (do not confuse this with "formatting" your SD card) determines how big of a computer record the camera will make for the image. DO NOT use the RAW setting unless you know what you are doing. A JPEG file is universal. FILE SIZE determines how large an image can print without PIXELATING (seeing the squares). Since most new cameras have at least 5MP (MEGAPIXELS or 5 million pixels per square inch) enlargements of 11x14 are easily made, UNLESS YOU HAVE USED THE ZOOM LENS ! !

• If you want a **DATE/TIME** to appear on your image, find and set this. (I don't do this because you can add them in editing, but they are tough to edit out). Digital cameras keep METADATA about when a picture was taken (as long as the date is set correctly in the menu of your camera, the data will get to your computer).

• Set your **AUTO SHUTOFF** (which will turn off the camera) longer if you pause a long time between pictures, or shorter to conserve battery if you wait between shots.

• Choose instant, on-LCD screen **REVIEW** if you like to check what your picture looks like as soon as you take it. As soon as you press the shutter button, the LCD SCREEN will display the picture you've taken for a few seconds (some cameras let you set how long the review lasts).

  » You can turn this feature off (most are factory set to show), particularly if you are taking pictures where time is important (sports/weddings).

  » If you want to take another picture right away, without having to turn off the feature, just gently touch your shutter button, and the on-LCD screen REVIEW will simply go away, and you can focus on the next shot.

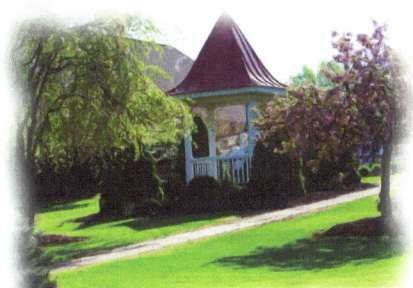

LANDSCAPE VIEW

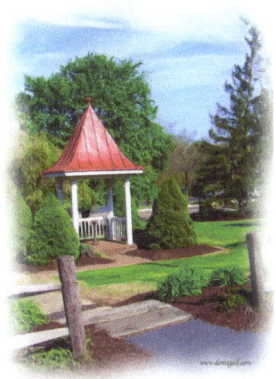

PORTRAIT VIEW

• Use the **AUTO ROTATE** feature if you tend to turn your camera sideways from the standard LANDSCAPE VIEW to a PORTRAIT shot. There will be a little cropping done within the camera by its program. Once you begin 'using' your pictures you will know whether or not this feature is one that you like; to start, I would use it.

• Turn **SOUNDS** off to conserve power and privacy! Some cameras let you set different sounds for different things: sounds are a matter of personal choice, but consider whether others will enjoy hearing the noise.

On most digital cameras there is a 'dial' or various buttons for some common "per shot" or **RECORDING** settings. You turn these on/off as you need them for a particular shot. Several are also available through the MENU feature, but are provided on a dial or button for speedy access. They include the following and more.

- IMAGE STABILIZATION shown either as 'IS' or several face outlines; the camera will accommodate "shake"

- LANDSCAPE shown as a mountain; meant for pictures of distant scenery (deep DEPTH OF FIELD, detail in distance)

- CLOSE UP shown as a little flower; meant for close ups of small things (only the object in focus, background blurs); check how close your camera will let you get (most say less than 28 inches, but won't let you get closer than 5; you can 'cheat' by using the zoom if you are careful; focus first, then zoom and re-focus)

- EXPOSURE shown as + and - with light and dark triangles; press + to add light into a dark shot, or press - to subtract light when it is too sunny

- FLASH, shown as a jagged arrow; lets you change the flash setting quickly (steps you through choices 1 by 1)

- TIMER shown as a clock; once you set it, you have a certain number of seconds before the shutter opens so you can jump into the shot (must set for each shot)

- REVIEW shown as an arrow pointing right; to see the pictures you have already taken (use compass to move once you are in review mode --- DELETE by pressing the button beside/with the trash can)

You may have more, but almost all cameras also have **SCENE** which will access a sub-menu of pictures that show particular kinds of shots that you might use.

SCENE SETTINGS are like miniature

programs within the camera to accommodate different
LIGHT, APERTURE, and SHUTTER SPEED situations. Since the
camera is all about light, the first thing it does is assess
the available light, then sets either APERTURE or SHUTTER
SPEED as the priority: basically making one dominant, and
setting the other to get enough light into the camera to
record an image. To me, this is the best 'magic' of digital
camera photography; if you can pick a scene, the camera
does all the work to set APERTURE and SHUTTER SPEED
(instead of you doing the work).

Manufacturers keep coming up with new scenes, but the
ones I think are useful to most people include these.

• PORTRAIT will blur the background while keeping the
person in sharp focus (be sure AUTOFOCUS locks on them)

• SPORT (or ACTION) is good for moving people or objects
so there is little blurring (don't use it if you want some)

• BEACH and/or SNOW is meant for very bright conditions
(or where there is a lot of reflection like in a white room)

• DOCUMENT is good for more than papers; I use it for
plaques at historical sites so I can remember details

• NIGHT SCENE is good for situations where buildings have
bright lights, but the sky is dark (use a tripod with this)

• CANDLE is meant for candlelight; it uses available
light and allows the warm colors to show; good for dim
conditions

• SUNSET allows the oranges, purples and pinks of a
beautiful sunset to be recorded (they wash out on AUTO)

There are still more things you can SET in your camera ! !

• MULTI-EXPOSURE, which usually looks like a stack of files, is useful for taking pictures of children, pets, and moving things/people because it will take a series of shots more quickly than you could possibly focus and shoot.

• BRACKET which you may not have, is often a menu item (not a button) and this 'takes' multiple pictures to have a "middle" image, with a 'less light' and 'more light' as well. This setting is very useful at church weddings where light is difficult to manage (don't use flash for the bride!).

• DISP is usually a button that brings up additional DISPLAY information; some of the time in has a '?' with it and it can access HELP material right on your LCD.

• AUTOFOCUS settings are available in the menu and usually include several options for how the camera 'locks onto' a subject. Choose carefully based on the kind of pictures you take. I rarely use face recognition, for example, because it takes so long to focus that the children are long gone. One of the most useful allows for multiple FOCUS POINTS for taking a group picture.

• And this section cannot be complete without explaining that: M means you will set everything Manually;
       S means that Shutter speed is to control the shot;
       A means that Aperture (f-stop) controls the shot;
and   P means you have a Program (formula for S and A to be used that you want to store for future use).

Try different SETTINGS, especially the SCENES for each shot, until you get experienced with them. Then, when you see the REVIEW image come up, you will learn to say, "oh, that would look better as ----- (whatever) scene."

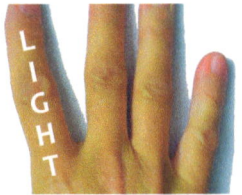

LIGHT
is what matters

more than anything else, because light is what is recorded by a digital camera on an image sensor behind the lens.

When you are choosing a camera, there are three critical aspects that directly affect the QUALITY of light captured.

» LENS is most important, but because many 'tiny' cameras have incredible processors, you can get an HD (high definition) image from a palm sized camera that has an 'equivalent' focal length. If you are serious about your images, though, invest in the best lens you can afford. The quality of the 'glass' and the range of its 'focal length' (distance to sensor and focusing depth of field) are crucial.

» SENSOR SIZE and its related FILE SIZE are next. If the sensor is small, not much data will be stored. You might have a lot of MEGAPIXELS, but if they are 'written' to a small sensor, the resulting FILE SIZE may limit print size, editing, etc. Choose the largest FILE SIZE (often called FINE) if you plan to do editing or large prints (>8x10).

» COLOR processing is the 'program' used by the camera to record the light. Just as different brands of television look different to us, so do different brands of cameras. It really is 'personal' preference.

As to whether you need a DSLR (digital single lens reflex), often considered "professional," that is up to you and what you want to photograph.

A DSLR is a specific type of camera where the lens and the sensor are in line with one another, and a mirror (that projects the image to the viewfinder) moves out of the way when you press the button to record/take the picture. It relates to the 35mm era, where the best shots kept the lens in line with the film. On a digital, the lens IS in line with the sensor, and what is shown on the display (LCD) or in the viewfinder is projected there based on data compiled by the sensor. A **BIG** difference is that a DSLR can have its lens changed ! ! ! If you do a variety of shoots that require top quality, then DSLR is the only way to go.

Back in BASICS we covered the color of light as **R**ed, **G**reen, and **B**lue. Most of us tend to think of it as ROYGBIV or the rainbow, because light put through a prism splits that way. But for 'recording' purposes, the colors are RGB.

Light reaches an object (say a red rose) and all colors EXCEPT red are absorbed; the red is reflected to our retina or the camera's image sensor, where it is recorded in the pattern of tone, PIXEL (square) by PIXEL (square) to store the image.

I emphasize this because the physics of light DIRECTLY AND TOTALLY affect your picture, because

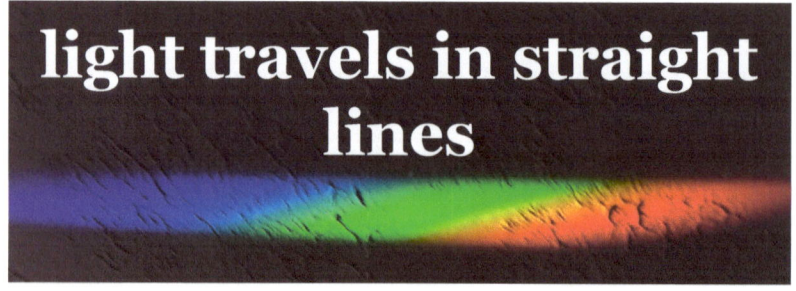

light travels in straight lines

but it bounces and reflects repeatedly.

My favorite technique is to shoot five pictures for every 'shot' you think is good until you get to know how your camera handles light into the lens. Simply take the shot you think you want, and then COMPASS it by taking four more: tip your camera the tiniest bit north (click-2), east (click-3), south (click-4), and west (click-5). Using this pattern lets you remember what worked and what didn't.

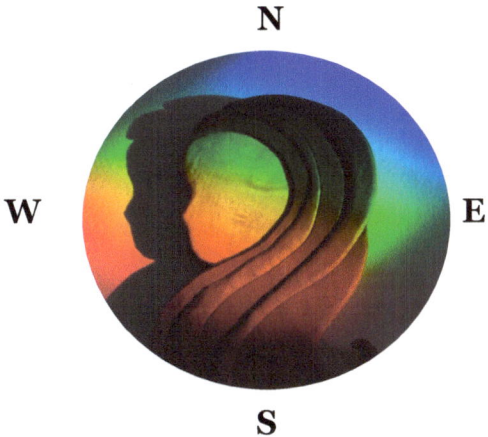

Once you get used to how light goes into your camera, you can move on to study the qualities, warmth and behaviors of it.

Light comes in three basic forms.
1. **Natural** -- light comes from the sun, travels in straight lines and reflects better than any other light.
2. **Ambient** or **artificial** -- light can be tungsten light bulbs which make things yellow/orange; fluorescent which casts green on everything (especially brides); as well as candles and other specialty light bulbs.
3. **Flash** -- which is a very specific, momentary burst of very white light. Flash can be IN the camera, ON the camera, or OFF the camera; either handheld, umbrella, or mounted.

The **TEMPERATURE** of light refers to how it feels to us and the corresponding COLOR of that light.

1. **Natural** -- light will have a 'temperature' that reflects the season of the year, so summer light is clear and bright, fall light tends to have orange in it, and winter light may lean toward blue. It depends on your climate; the light will favor the colors of the season.

2. **Ambient** or **artificial** --is going to have the temperature of its color, where we feel that yellows, oranges and reds are warm, and blues and greens are cool. Halogen light, which is very bright may add a tint of purple to an image and will 'warm' it or 'cool' it depending on the other colors in the situation.

3. **Flash** -- provides a very sharp image and because it is sudden, rarely is seen as having a temperature.

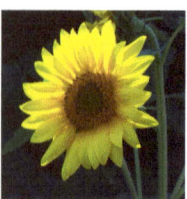 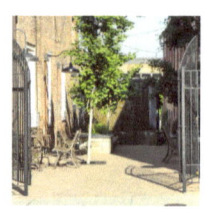 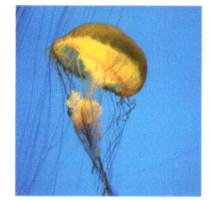 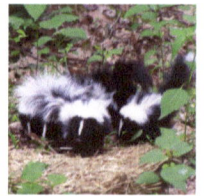

- warm light is yellow or orange
- cool light is blue or bright white
- diffuse light (like near dawn and dusk, after a rain, or in the fog) is considered the very best light for pictures because there are NO clear shadows on the subject
- bright light (high noon, the beach, fresh snow with sun) is the most difficult light to shoot, but can be worth the work to manage the harsh shadows it creates
- underwater light 'records' as blue (though our eyes correct for this, the camera will not)
- strong sunlight that is filtered with an ultraviolet (UV) filter will result in sharper edges on objects, bluer skies, and more clear greens (and the filter protects your lens)

We refer to the QUALITY of light, and frequently say

"when the light is right, shoot"

because perfect light makes an amazing picture;
a picture that doesn't require any editing to
achieve a compelling image
or luminous effect.

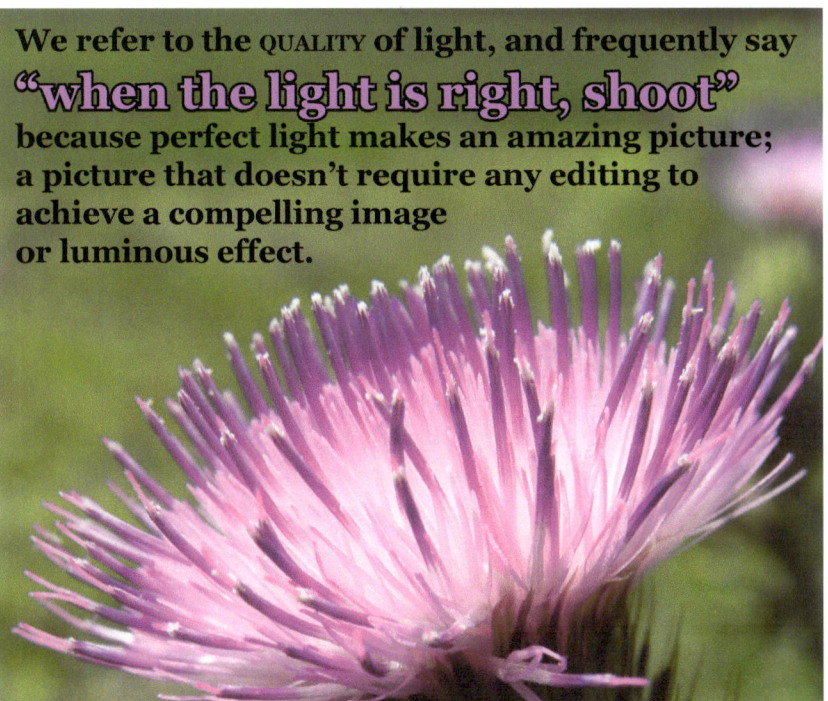

The light that gets into the camera is controlled by how
long the **S**hutter is held open (SHUTTER SPEED) and the
size of the iris or **A**perture (F-STOP where the higher
the number the smaller the iris opening). The subject or
scene you are trying to capture often sets one of these,
and then you have to work with the other. Whenever
possible use the SCENE SETTINGS of your camera until you
are proficient because manually manipulating **S** or **A**
requires more training than this short book can provide.
But in general, while you learn:

- if you have to extend the **S**hutter speed in low light,
  make sure you set the camera on a tripod or a beanbag;
- if you need a deep DEPTH OF FIELD, use F-STOP 11 or
  higher, set a long Shutter speed, and use a tripod;
- take as many pictures as the subject and time allows,
  varying the settings (choose the best picture later).

TOO MUCH LIGHT IS NOT AS COMMON AS TOO LITTLE LIGHT.

- Simply adding a UV filter on your lens will reduce the 'available' light into the camera up to 30%. This means that either the SHUTTER SPEED or APERTURE must change dramatically (versus an unfiltered reading).

- Using the telephoto ZOOM on your camera reduces light into the lens because it lengthens the FOCAL LENGTH and 'shrinks' the available lens opening. It also INCREASES your risk of BLUR because:
  » 1) the lens is usually open longer; and
  » 2) on zoom, movement is as magnified as the image, so the smallest hand tremor moves the frame!

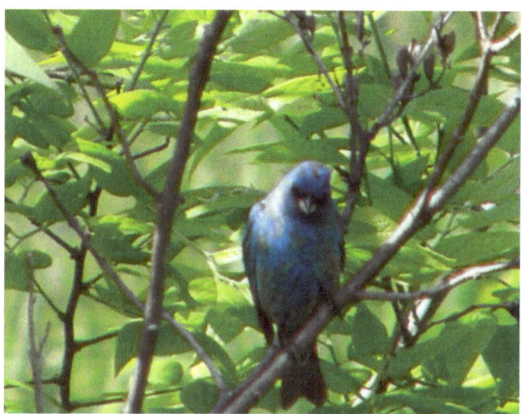

This telephoto of an indigo bunting is a little bit blurry. It is much better to get a crisp shot, with the indigo in FOCUS but not as close like below.

If the detail is there and crisp, you can edit to CROP for the closer picture (as long as the image/ FILE SIZE is large enough to NOT PIXELATE).

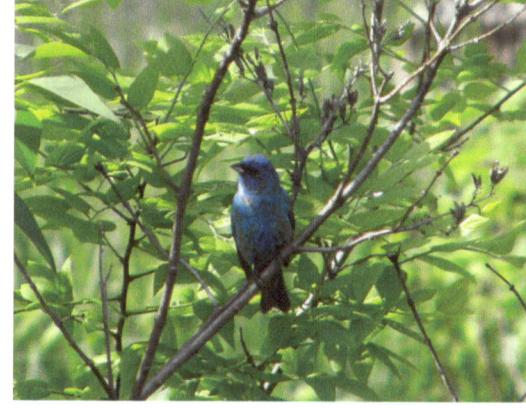

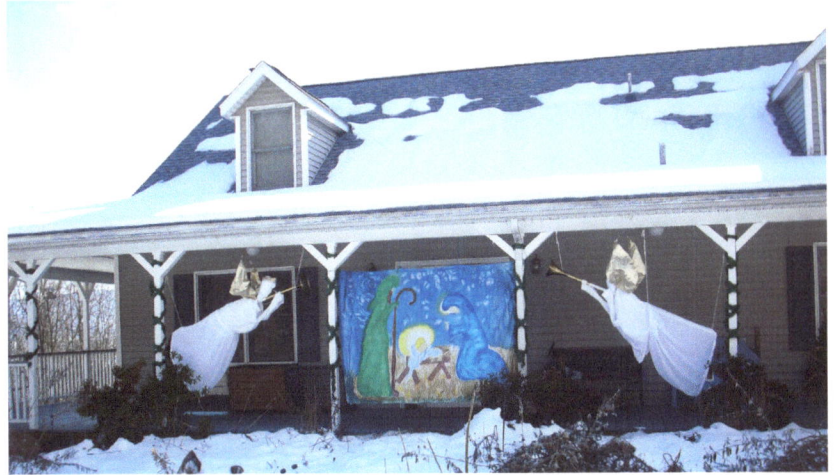

For those situations where the image is, or will be, too dark, your camera has an entire arsenal of SETTINGS that help you get more light on the subject.

• Increase the EXPOSURE (+ button if you have one).

• Boost the **ISO** SETTING which makes the sensor record more light per PIXEL. ISO is a light sensitivity setting that relates to film, but which we still use with the digital camera. ISO in film meant that an ISO of 200 gave you a good detailed image (but you had to have good light in the scene, or use a flash); an ISO of 800 let you take a picture inside your home without a flash (but the resulting print usually had a 'GRAINY' appearance). The same is true in digital; a higher ISO will let in more light, but may add NOISE (a grainy look) to your printed image especially if it is enlarged in any way.

• Use the FLASH judiciously; most only reach 8-12 feet out, and if the camera thinks the flash is going to reach your subject, it will have set the SHUTTER SPEED (or APERTURE) accordingly and your shot will be dark.

Using a flash to add light to your image is one way to be certain that you have good FOCUS and enough DEPTH OF FIELD to show everything you want to capture.

- the flash built into the camera is perfect for 'stopping' action but NOT for illuminating deep shadows.
  » AUTO lets the camera program decide whether to fire;
  » RED EYE FLASH provides an extra flash before the shutter opens to cause the eye pupils to close some;
  » FILL FLASH forces the flash to fire to add light to the scene (a person wearing a hat will benefit from this)

- a 'HOTSHOE' (mounted-on-the-camera) flash is great if it is powerful and can be adjusted to bounce off the ceiling down onto the subject.

- an 'OFF CAMERA' flash that you aim to bounce light onto your subject is perhaps the best option.

- you can turn a 'HOTSHOE' flash into an 'OFF CAMERA' flash by buying a special cord to attach between the flash and the camera (you can also get a frame that moves the flash up and off the camera with angle adjustments).

- you DON'T need an 'umbrella' flash for portraits, but if that is what you will be doing a lot of, these are becoming less expensive (the bulb is costly so don't fire it for practice).

- you can get interesting effects by placing colored glass or a mirror in front of the built-in flash; use a soda or other bottle and simply hold it there while your flash goes off (a tripod really helps with this trick).

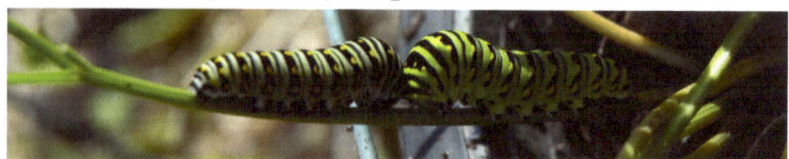

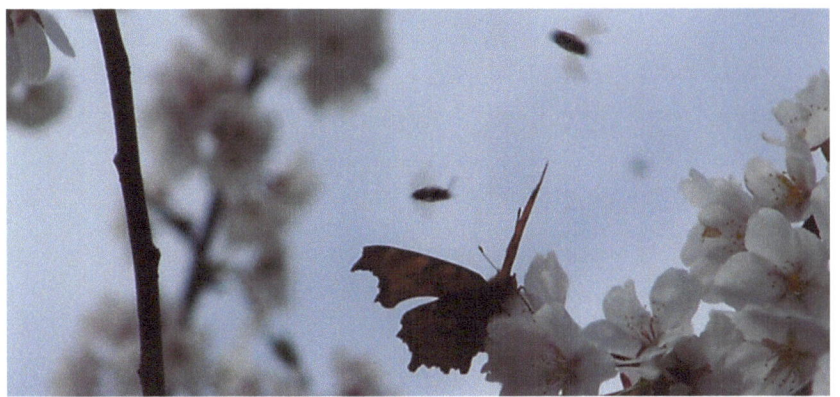

There are some other things you can do to add light to your scene:

    » open the curtains to let in more natural light;
    » turn on lamps and overhead lights (move them around to get the light where you need it);
    » use a piece of white FOAMCORE board, or other white object (with a matte surface, not shiny) to 'reflect' some of the available light (make sure it is white or it will cast color on your subject --- a different technique entirely)
    » use an acrylic hand-held mirror, with or without a flashlight, to add light to a particular part of the scene.

BUT remember, too much light means too little detail so CHOOSE TOO DARK an image (over too light), because, editing affords a final opportunity to add light to your image. If it is already too bright (below left), the light has BURNED OUT the detail you cannot recreate!

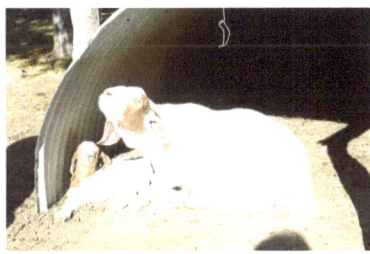
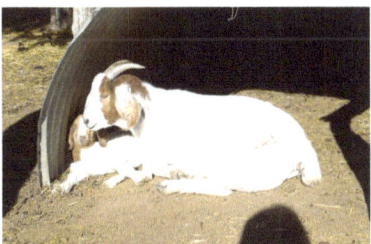

The MENU setting for WHITE BALANCE (which is different than the +/- button to increase or decrease EXPOSURE) can help when your AUTO setting doesn't give you the clarity of white (or colors) that you want. Usually you will see the following choices under WHITE BALANCE in the menu.

- DAYLIGHT or SUNNY, that you might use if the day is extremely bright, which if not corrected can result in whited out areas. (The BEACH scene might also help).

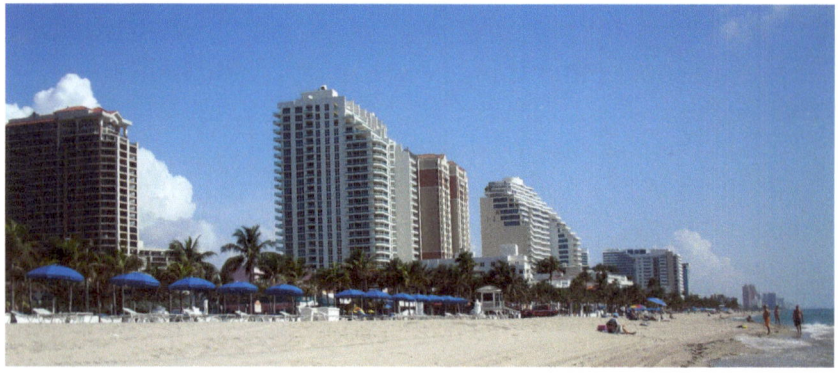

- FLUORESCENT, where there are lots of them like in a school, church hall, or office building, which if not corrected, may have a green cast on white things like the bride's dress. (AUTO only compensates for some, not a lot of FLUORESCENT light fixtures.)

- INCANDESCENT like the original light bulbs with the filament in them, which if not corrected can add an orange or yellow cast to the entire picture. (Not the new energy friendly ones, which are closer to natural light).

- CLOUDY may be an option, which you can use to reduce gray in the image. Generally the light on a cloudy day is nice and diffuse, so I rarely use this option.

- Under FLASH, you will have the settings mentioned earlier: AUTO, RED EYE, and FILL.

To better demonstrate WHITE BALANCE, if you had to set it yourself all the time, I turned off AUTO on my DSLR to see an item in different light settings. It is graphic art (black dots applied to a white board), hung on a white wall. Below are uncorrected images.

natural light   fluorescent   tungsten

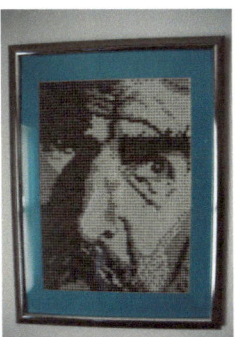 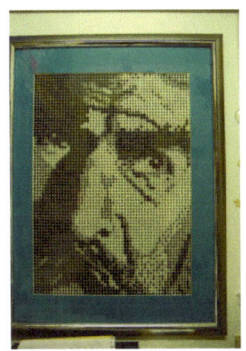 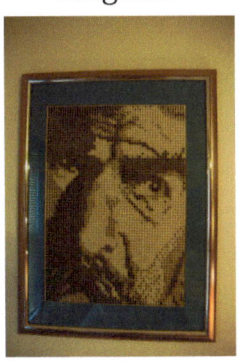

Regardless of the color (or warmth) of the light, the amount of light that gets into the camera is controlled by how long the **S**hutter is held open (SHUTTER SPEED) and the size of the iris or **A**perture (F-STOP). The subject or scene you are trying to capture often sets one of these as the PRIORITY, and then determines the other based on the brightness of the scene.

You can better control things on your own if you know:

a speedy shutter STOPS action
but lets in less light

a small opening
(f-stop 11 or 16) gives more detail (DOF)
but lets in less light

So, unless it is a really bright scene, or you can use a flash that reaches the subject, you will have to sacrifice either speed or detail (DEPTH OF FIELD). Get as much in focus as you can, using a tripod to extend shutter time, because you can't add detail (but you can edit to blur it out).

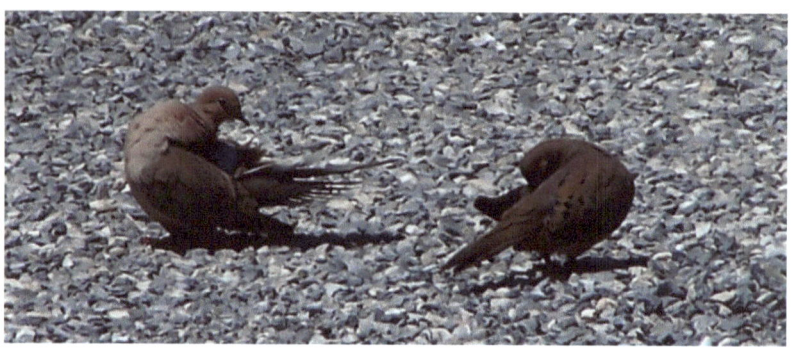

SIMPLY,
ACTIVELY, CONTROL LIGHT and
you will have success with every picture that you take ! ! !

As long as you think about 'how' the light is reflecting into the camera, you will be able to figure out how to use the situation, and light, to get the picture you desire. This means

the DIRECTION of light
onto the subject also matters.

- front light is good for architecture, NOT for faces.
- back light (on/behind the subject) means the camera gives a very dark image unless a fill or forced flash is used to compensate for the shadows.
- side lighting will cast shadow to the other half of an object or face, which can be nice if it is what you desire.
- diffuse lighting, where light is all around the subject, is the BEST because the camera can read it the easiest.

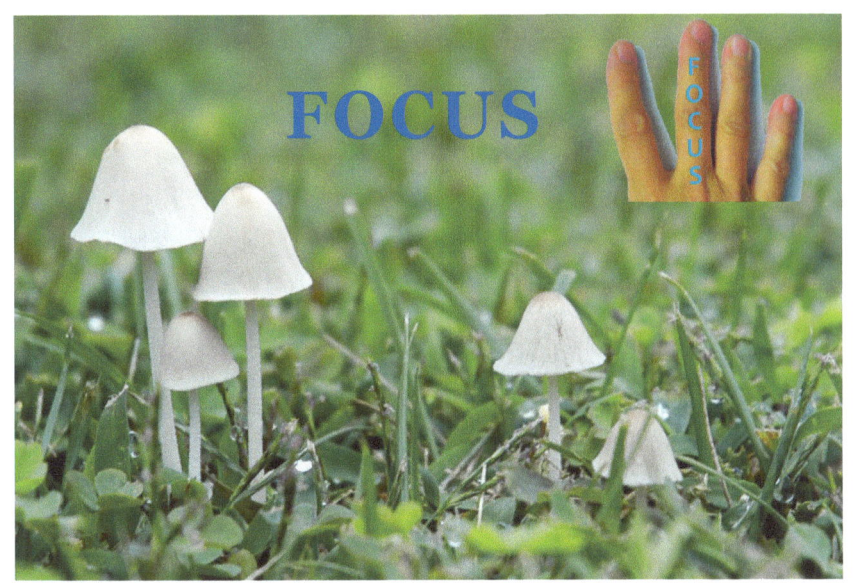

FOCUS provides clarity in two very different ways in photography.

FIRST, the subject of your photo must be in-focus, with crisp edges, no blur, and enough DEPTH OF FIELD that your subject is 'all in focus' and well presented to the viewer. None of this is easy or, despite the label AUTOFOCUS on your camera, automatic. It requires practice, repetition and often, multiple shots of the subject.

SECOND, you, as a photographer, must have a clear idea of what you want the SUBJECT (focus), or FOCAL POINT, of your picture to be. I will cover composing your shot to 'focus' on something in the next section but raise the idea here because it greatly affects the use of DEPTH OF FIELD.

Consider the mushrooms on this page. Since they were the subject of my shot, I got down on the ground so that I did not distort them by shooting from above. I 'stopped' down (F-STOP 11) so that all the mushrooms were in focus in the shot, but didn't worry that most of the grass would blur out. In fact, that adds to the resulting image by allowing the eye to go right to the mushrooms.

To a certain extent, I am using focus, and the lack of focus (blur) to get the viewer to FOCUS on what I want. Again, this is partly a composition issue, but if you don't understand the way that the camera FOCUSES first, your ability to COMPOSE the shot will be limited.

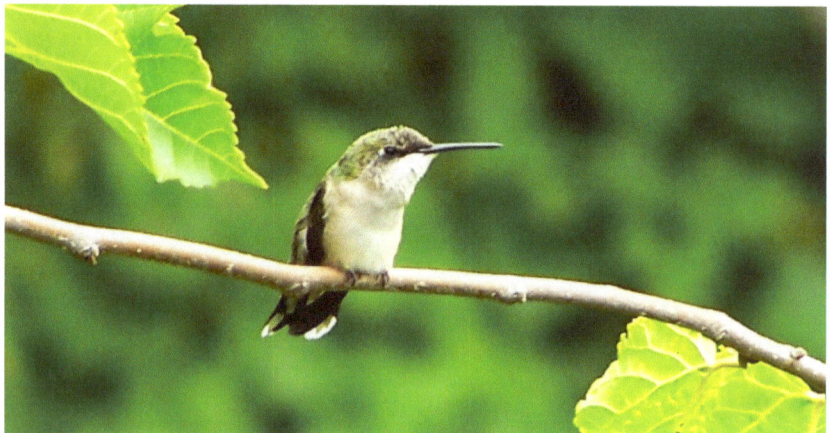

When you press the shutter button on your camera only half-way, the ANGLES for AUTOFOCUS will appear, usually as white, yellow or red UNTIL the program finds an object and calculates FOCUS. Once the camera locks onto the object and calculates focus, the ANGLES turn green, and if sound is ON, you hear a beep indicating that you can press the shutter button the rest of the way to RECORD the shot.

How your particular camera locks onto a subject, or FOCUSES, can frustrate you until you get used to it.

First, practice using AUTOFOCUS with a single AUTOFOCUS FRAME (default setting) and a single subject. Take pictures really fast and notice what you get when you don't use the HALF press of the shutter button to allow the camera to AUTOFOCUS.

If the light is really bright and the subject is large, you might have a fine picture. If the light is not bright, the subject smaller, or the camera simply didn't have time to do its job, there is sure to be BLUR.

Perhaps, looking at your two-inch by three-inch LCD (liquid crystal display), you don't see any blur? Take the time to go to your computer and look at the pictures on-screen there. The LCD on the camera can seem just fine because the PIXELS are compressed to such a small area that sharpness isn't an issue, but when you see the image on your computer, there is significant blurring.

Take pictures of things you like so that you get the 'feel' for how your camera 'locks onto' a subject. I shoot a lot of butterfly images. With trial and error, I know to 'aim' slightly off the butterfly when the light is a certain way, not only because of the way my camera focuses, but because nature provides camouflage that gives the camera lots of trouble 'reading' a butterfly (or caterpillar, or bird).

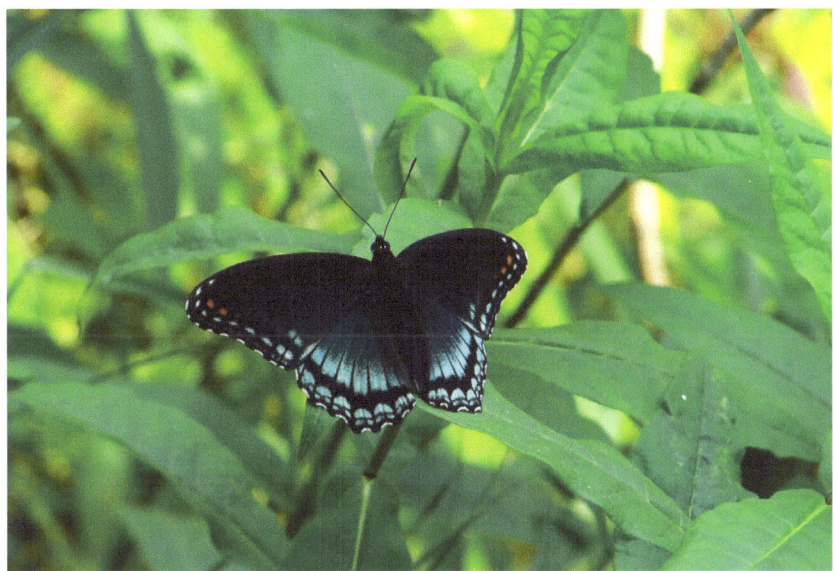

Practice, practice, practice

using AUTOFOCUS, because getting the subject of your image sharply FOCUSED is the single most important step in taking a picture. Unless you are looking for a soft focus portrait, which is best done with a SCENE or a filter, sharp detail of the subject must be there in the image file.

- lock onto a person's eyes, not their nose
- lock onto the baby's face, not their hands
- lock onto the pistil in the flower, not the petal
- lock onto the center of a building, not the closest point

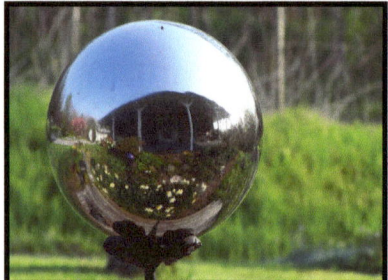 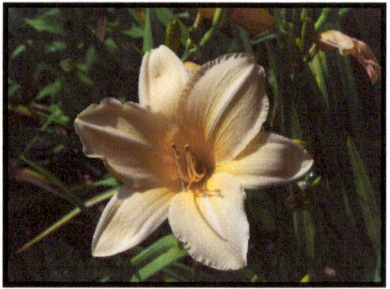

ROUND OBJECTS like birds, globes, and a baby's face are difficult to AUTOFOCUS but if you practices and shift your camera the tiniest bit off angle (rather than straight on to the subject) you will succeed.

BRIGHTLY LIT OBJECTS like flowers in sunlight, can be difficult to AUTOFOCUS unless you are shooting at the same level as the flower. Squat down, lie down, or use a tripod to get in a direct line with your subject.

FUR ON CREATURES like your pet can confuse the AUTOFOCUS. Add light to the situation (but try not to use the FLASH).

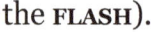

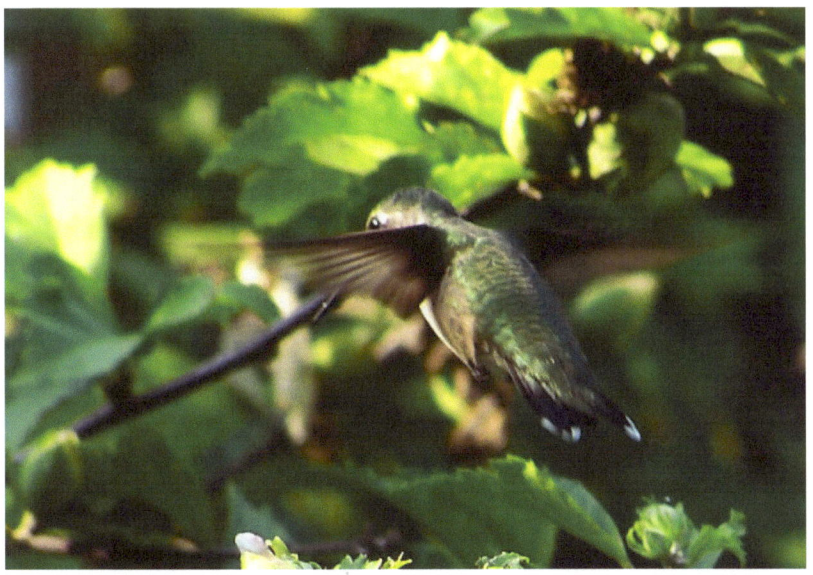

MOVING OBJECTS like birds or children rarely **AUTOFOCUS**.

- use an appropriate **SCENE SETTING** (sport or action) which will set the shutter speed at 1/200th or faster to stop the action and capture the subject without **BLUR**

- you can **PRE-FOCUS** on the spot of an anticipated moving object (a hummingbird or the winner at the finish line at a sporting event), making sure that the **DEPTH OF FIELD** will be adequate for the bird or winner, and then stay with the button pressed **HALFWAY,** waiting to **SNAP** until the subject is in the frame.

- group pictures almost always have someone moving, but that motion is usually less of a problem than getting all of the faces in **FOCUS**. Some cameras include **FACE RECOGNITION** capability; others have settings for **MULTIPLE AUTOFOCUS FRAMES** that allow the camera to lock onto two (or more) people or objects; this can help quite a bit at events where more than one person will be in the shot.

Start with **SHARP FOCUS** for the **SUBJECT** of a photo and you'll have the basis for a perfect picture. If the subject is NOT sharply in focus to start with, there is little that you can do to save the shot. Some new computer programs can add SHARPENING but, beware, because all that these programs do is use a formula to add pixels in places to create 'crisper' edges within the existing image. Perhaps there are situations, like a large format image file that will be printed small, where this will work for you. Or perhaps, your image is primarily for 'MEMORY PROMPTING' and the slight variance won't matter. I recommend getting the shot IN FOCUS to start with if at all possible.

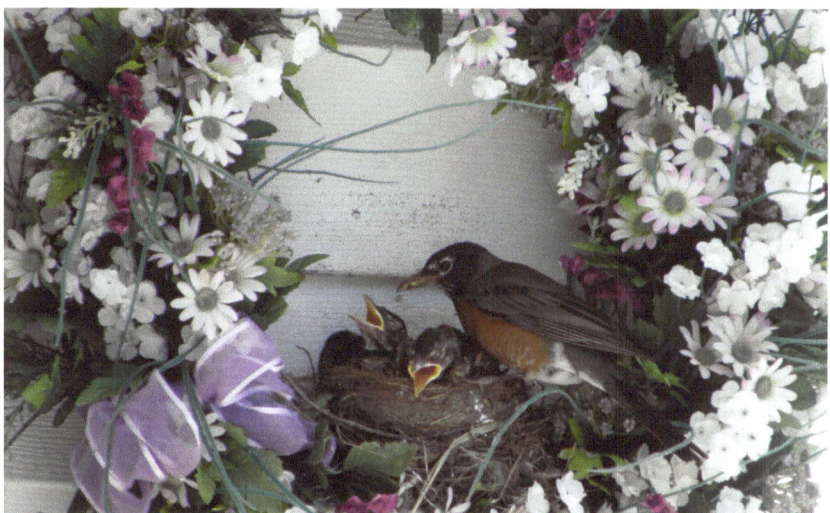

Focusing manually is possible on many cameras, but should be reserved for those situations where you cannot get the camera to FOCUS; either because you are too close to the subject, or you are choosing a tiny point among many points (a blue butterfly among the clover). MANUAL FOCUS techniques are specific to each BRAND and MODEL of camera, so if you want to try it, check your instructions and take time to practice.

TELEPHOTO ZOOM (the T on the right of a rocker button with a W for wide angle on the left) seriously affects FOCUS. There are two kinds of zoom. OPTICAL ZOOM works just like a telescope; it extends the lens to 'get closer' to the subject. DIGITAL ZOOM is a computer program that simply crops the image recorded at maximum OPTICAL ZOOM and enlarges it like a computer program would.

On ZOOM, the tiniest movement of the camera when you press the shutter button will result in BLUR because, just like telephoto enlarges the subject, telephoto magnifies movement. So whenever possible, get closer to the subject and skip the ZOOM. If you need to zoom, use a tripod or lean against a solid object like a wall, table, or car.

ZOOM greatly affects **FOCAL LENGTH** which I will explain because so many small digital cameras have the EQUIVALENT of changing lenses like you would with a DSLR. The distance from the LENS (cornea) of the camera to the IMAGE SENSOR (retina) inside the camera is the FOCAL LENGTH. Think of it as a sideways cone, similar to the cone that happens when light passes through the lens of our eye to the retina behind it.

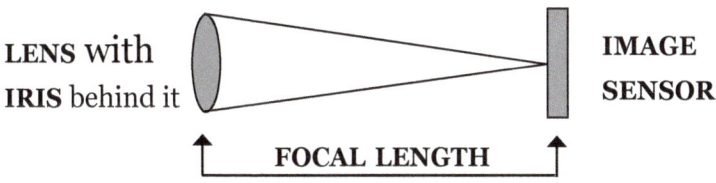

The focal length is the measured distance (in millimeters) and, just like with our vision, results in a particular **shape** of cone that affects the depth of detail focused on the image sensor.

The distance that light travels between the lens and the image sensor affects how much DETAIL there will be in the image because, the further light has to travel, the less precise it is. The TYPE OF LENS also affects the QUANTITY, and QUALITY, of light that goes through it.

WIDE ANGLE LENS - FOCAL LENGTH 28-35 mm distorts, like looking into a fishbowl

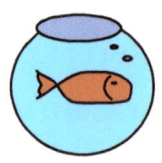

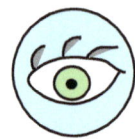

NORMAL LENS - FOCAL LENGTH 45-60 mm is like vision (to have details requires light)

TELEPHOTO LENS - FOCAL LENGTH 70-135 mm softens everything except the subject focused upon

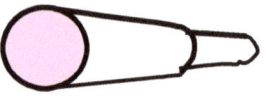

So the FOCAL LENGTH of the lens, which also dictates the shape or type of lens, affects how much will be IN FOCUS in front of and behind the object that you lock onto with AUTOFOCUS.

This is DEPTH OF FIELD (DOF) for your image. With WIDE ANGLE and TELEPHOTO the amount in FOCUS will be limited to pixels right in front of and right behind your subject; everything else will BLUR out (appear as smeary color).

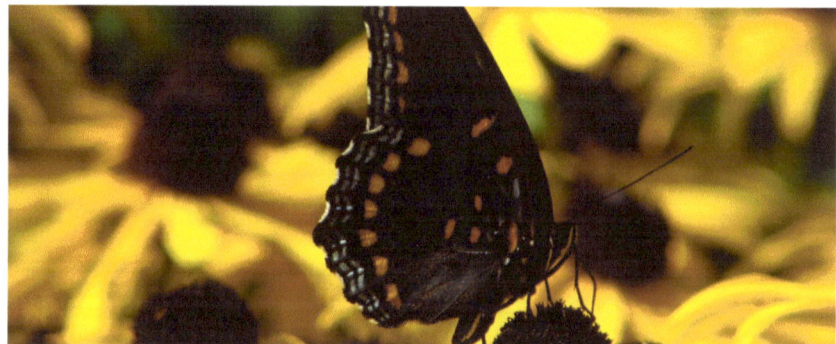

With a **NORMAL** lens, you have control over
how much is IN FOCUS

in front of and behind your subject because the shape of
the lens is not an issue. What IS an issue is the **QUANTITY**
of light, and the **QUALITY** (shape) of the cone created by
the **F-STOP SETTING**.

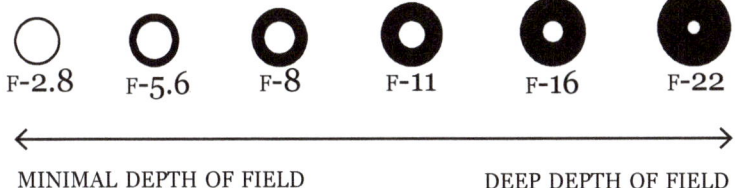

F-2.8   F-5.6   F-8   F-11   F-16   F-22

⟵————————————————————————————⟶
MINIMAL DEPTH OF FIELD   DEEP DEPTH OF FIELD

FIRST, QUANTITY -- the easiest way to let more light into
the camera is to have the shutter open longer (**SHUTTER
SPEED** is slow, like 1/60th of a second). This does risk
BLUR from movement (an out-of-focus appearance), but if
you use a tripod or are steady, you get more light, which
will mean more details, more **DEPTH OF FIELD (DOF)**.

SECOND, QUALITY -- the quality of light is determined
by the shape of the cone of light created by the **IRIS** of
the camera. Also known as **APERTURE** or **F-STOP**, light
that reaches the **IMAGE SENSOR** will have more **DEPTH OF
FIELD** if the cone is **NORMAL** in shape rather than shallow
or steep. This cone is shaped by the **OPENING** size of the
IRIS. For lots of detail, as in a landscape picture, a small
opening (pupil constricted) is required. This would be a
HIGH F number like **F-11, F-16, OR F-22**.

A large opening (pupil dilated) would be appropriate for
close-ups where the background would distract. This
would be a **LOW F** number like **F-2.8, F-5.6, OR F-8**.

Getting everything **IN-FOCUS** that you want to have
IN FOCUS is a balancing act. If you want lots of detail, deep
into the image, AVOID telephoto and wide angle lenses.
Once that is controlled, you must decide whether there
is enough available light to support an F-STOP of 11 or
more (to capture more detail). If a slow shutter speed
can be used, do so, otherwise you will have to go back to
the section on light to see what other TRICKS you can use
to get more light into the camera (ISO, WHITE BALANCE,
EXPOSURE, SCENE SETTINGS).

Just remember to decide what the subject is and how
much DEPTH OF FIELD around the subject you want FIRST.
Then you can use SCENE SETTINGS, manually adjust
SHUTTER SPEED, or manually adjust APERTURE to get as
much in focus as you want.

Like any balancing act, choices have to be made. If there
is a lot of available light, the balancing is easier. If there
isn't a lot of available light (at a school concert), the use
of a MONOPOD (one-legged tri-pod) may be the only way to
capture your child playing their instrument.

Be clear about what you want the SUBJECT of your picture
to be, and then get that subject in FOCUS with enough
DEPTH OF FIELD (fore and aft) to convey your vision.

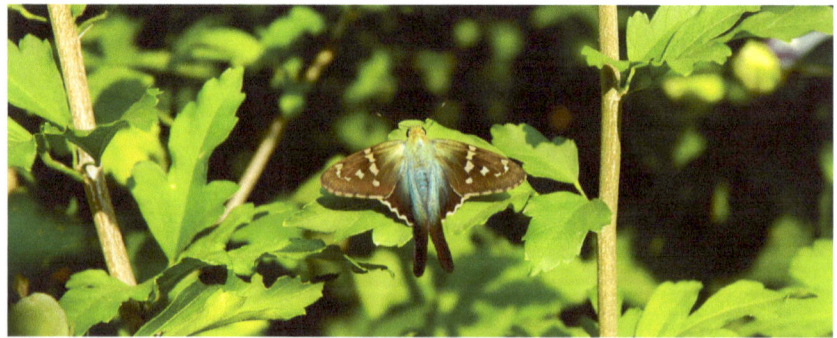

COMPOSITION
is your vision
of the scene; what you want the viewer to focus upon.

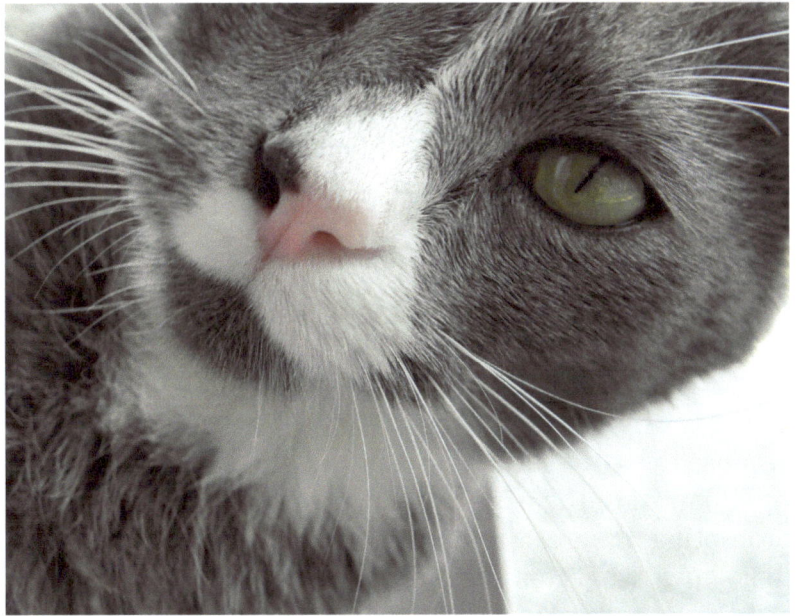

As long as your subject is in focus, you can always EDIT the image to add or subtract things that appear in it so that it better matches your vision, but I firmly believe that the less editing you have to do, the better. You can't always get what you want after the fact. The most valuable point of a digital camera is your ability to take hundreds of shots with NO additional expense. You can throw 99 away and keep the one that 'works' best.

That said, if you are a perfectionist, or an 'edit' type, who wants to 'do more' the images, I **still** think you should start with the best possible COMPOSITION.

COMPOSITION is influenced by the 5 W's of reporting:
- **WHO** will view the picture you are going to take
- **WHAT** you are photographing (portrait, place, or project)
- **WHERE** you will take the picture (affects available lighting and the settings for **DEPTH OF FIELD**)
- **WHEN** you will take the picture (time of day)
- **WHY** you are taking the picture (may decide the other 4)

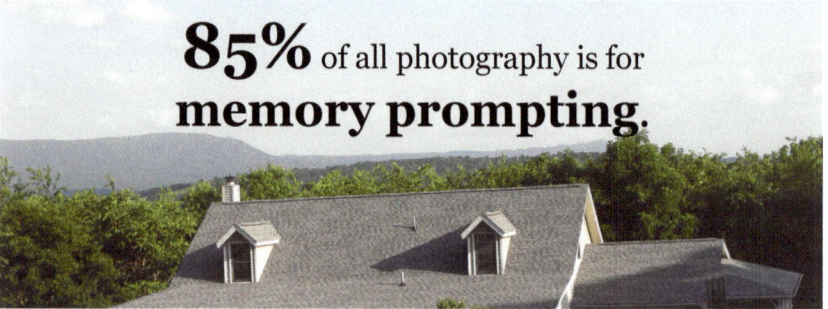

85% of all photography is for
memory prompting.

If that is why you are taking pictures, you can really relax because the **AUTO** setting or your preferred **SCENE SETTINGS** will do most of the work, 80% of the time. For memory prompting, the most important composition is the one that shows what was going on, and who was there. A good clear picture (though we seem to accept blurry for memory) with everyone in the frame, is what you need.

The remaining **15%** covers amateurs & professionals who:

- create a **record** of a person, project, or event (a portrait, a construction site, a wedding or party);

- create an **advertisement** or persuasive piece (in a magazine or for an on-line auction site);

- create a **statement** of beauty, society or other aesthetic (scenery, architecture, cuisine, and pure art).

Photographs that we enjoy looking at are the ones that

draw our eye to the subject

and this is easily done by following some universal rules
of design. The first one may already be available as a
guide in your camera; it is called the Rule of Thirds, and
looks like a grid or TIC-TAC-TOE board.

You put your subject on
one of the four points
where the lines intersect
(NOT inside any of the
spaces).

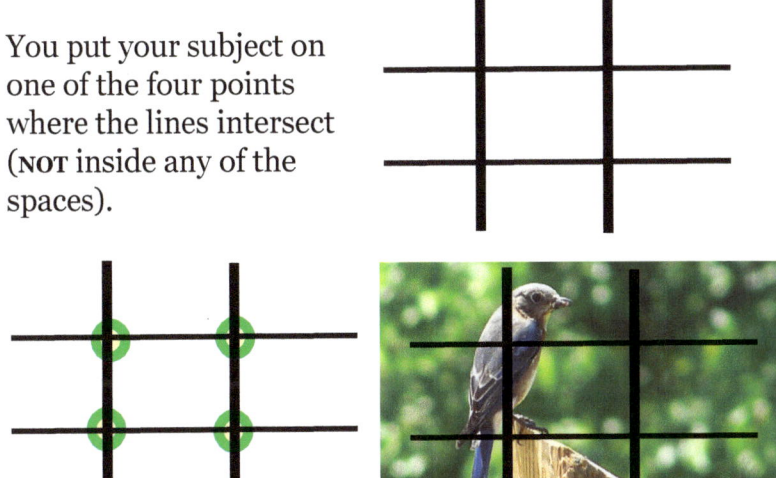

When you take the picture, make sure you have adequate
FRAME around it, especially if your camera 'shifts' a bit
between LCD and final image. Also, be aware that most
programs and all printers will CROP some portion of your
image to translate it from the format of your camera to
a computer or printer. It is better to have a some FRAME
around your subject than to cut a person in half at the
edge of your family or group photo.

Get IN LINE with the subject and take time to really SEE
what is actually in the frame. Remember, our brain edits
stuff out! Take the time to notice that power line!

prize winning pictures

are the ones that convey a FEELING in addition to clarity. How we capture feeling is by taking shots of people, creatures and places in an UN-STAGED way. Capture natural facial expressions rather than posed 'cheese' smiles. Get down on the floor with the baby and stay there long enough to capture them totally absorbed in a toy. Arrange objects like you are a world class designer (use magazines for ideas), and just generally visualize OUTSIDE THE FRAME.

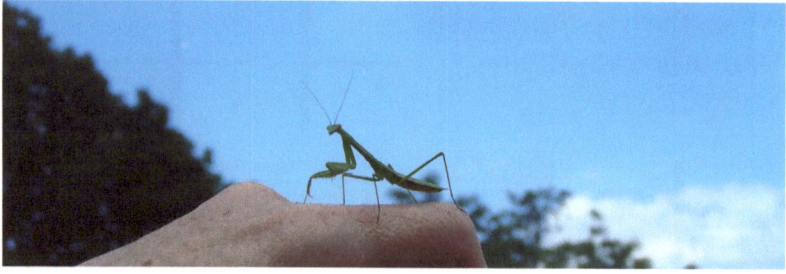

Once you have spent time trying these things with the RULE OF THIRDS, you can learn the more advanced kinds of frames: the GOLDEN ones.

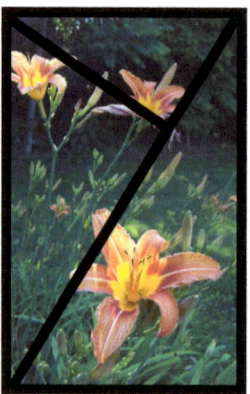

The GOLDEN TRIANGLE is meant to handle three subjects of nearly equal size (in real size, or in perspective), each one placed inside a triangle. The FRAME is divided in half diagonally, then from the corner to a right angle into the first line. The large triangle can be at any corner, portrait format (left) or landscape format (below).

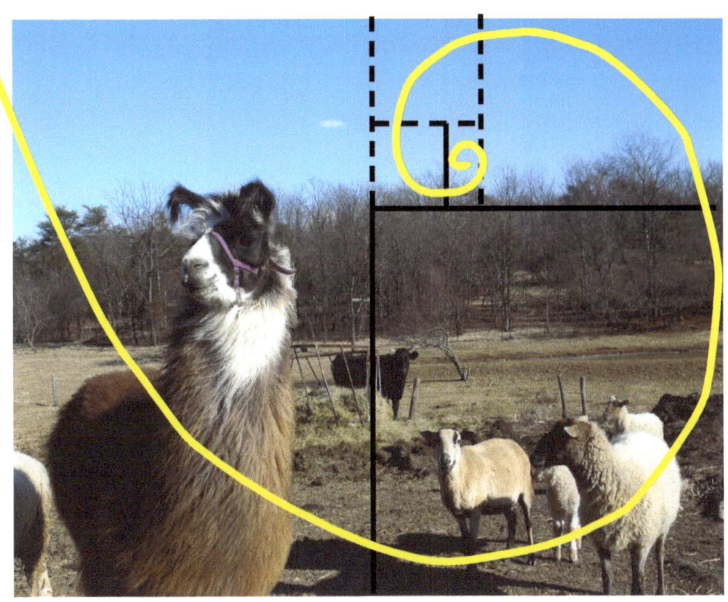

The GOLDEN RECTANGLE is another frame that is very useful for images of nature. It is a rectangle that is repeatedly divided using the DIVINE PROPORTION, also known as PHI or ϕ (1.618) to create another rectangle and a square. This repeats again and again, always at PHI. This is the same as a nautilus shell's chambers, or the unfurling of a fern (Fibonacci's sequence).

The application of the DIVINE PROPORTION to something you are composing takes practice, but it is worth it. Many famous logo's (and my g) satisfy PHI proportions. The human face and the Eiffel tower reflect it as well.

All three frames are based upon the geometry of the DIVINE PROPORTION, and understanding it goes a long way toward taking better pictures. Spend time looking at images in magazines, on display, and with friends so that you begin to assess what you like and don't in the organization and arrangement of the objects in the frame.

COMPOSITION is enhanced by the use of color, lines, and reflection of the **OBJECTS IN THE SHOT** to pull the eye toward the subject of the picture.

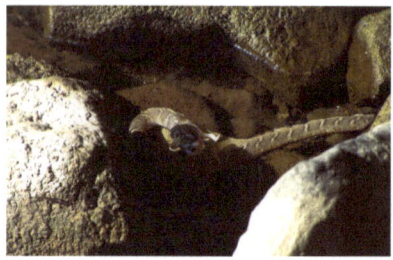

If there is a 'natural' frame in the shot, like a window or these rocks, use it to border the subject (snake).

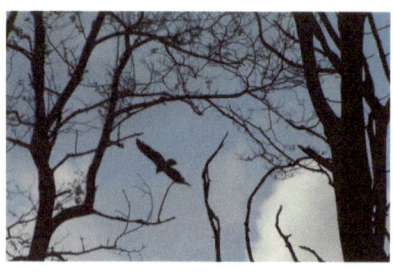

If you see strong lines in your frame, like a fence, branches or a shoreline, use them to accent your subject.

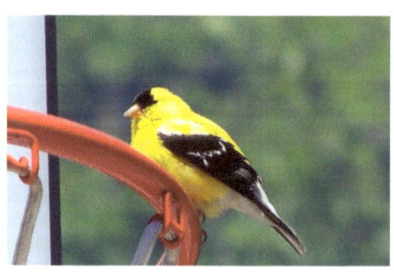

Look for sweeping lines, curves, and colors using the viewfinder or your hands held in "movie frame."

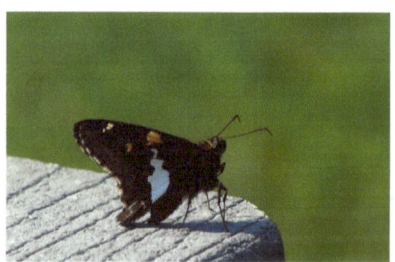

Look for shapes that repeat, like the angle of the wing and the deck.

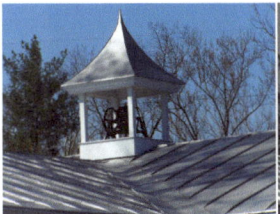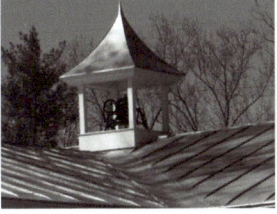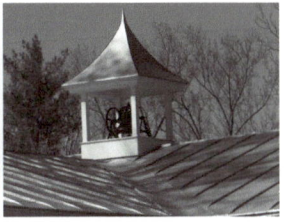

With a digital camera you can take **BLACK AND WHITE** images simply by choosing that setting. Some subjects and situations lend themselves to this better than others: portraits, zebras, bridges, and old automobiles for example. If you like **BLACK AND WHITE,** use the **SETTING** on the camera, rather than editing it to **B/W** later, so you can make contrast and lighting adjustments at the site. Also take a color image, so you have the option of **EDITING** to **BLACK AND WHITE,** (center) or to **GRAYSCALE** (right) which will be subtly different.

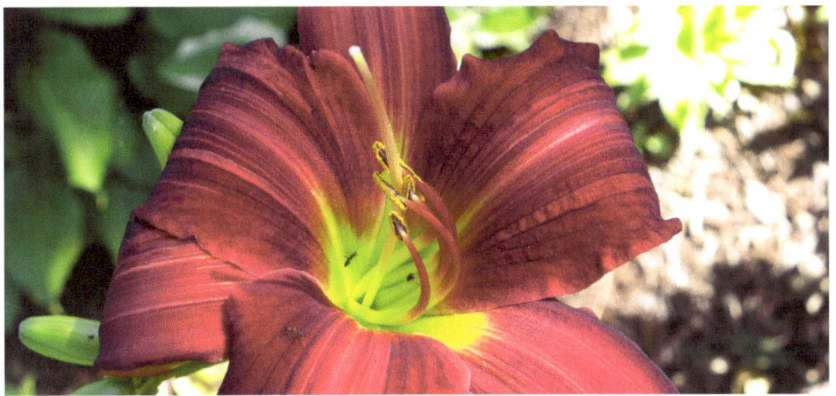

Strong color, rather than its absence in B/W, can provide contrast, pulling the eye to the subject. This works when photographing flowers: get down low to put the sky behind the flower; or wait until dusk when the grass is rich green and tilt the lens for a lush green background.

In portrait taking, have everyone **EXCEPT** THE NEW BABY wear denim blue and have the baby in bright colors.

Above all, take the shot that speaks to you, and what you want the viewer to see. DIVINE PROPORTION and color are wonderful to understand so that you get a feel for what works, but it is never meant to dominate your vision.

Unique angles and other 'tricks' are just that if the resulting image looks staged. Share a message, save a memory, or suggest an idea with your composition, and you will feel like a prize winning photographer every time!

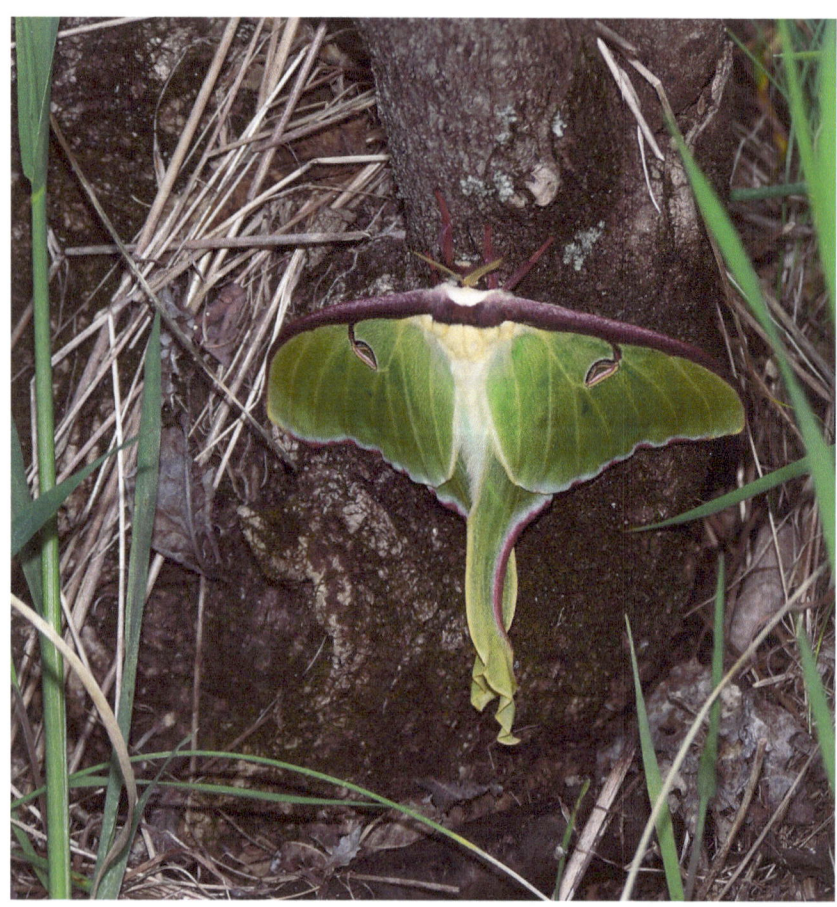

EDITING
is changing
an image

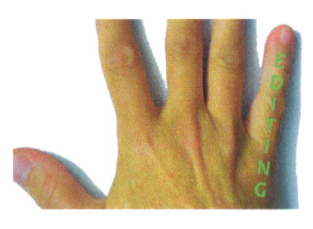

to add, subtract, fix, or enhance something in the frame after the image file has been recorded. Some digital cameras have editing software inside the camera. Photo kiosks and online sites usually have basic editing on-screen before you order a print. Software for your computer, to upload and edit images, comes with most cameras. And if you are a true editing enthusiast, you have a lot of programs that can be purchased (inexpensively or costly) to enhance or change an image.

Whether to edit, and how much to edit is a personal choice. I am most likely to edit images taken at an event that won't happen again, like a wedding or the hatching of a butterfly chrysalis. Those situations (images) cannot be recreated, and the first ones might benefit from some touch-up. Editing, then is worth knowing about.

To simplify discussion of it, I am going to divide editing into the things that I consider FORMAT changes, and the things that involve ARTISTIC changes.

FORMAT changes include any change to the image
that leaves the PIXEL 'content' basically the same.

ARTISTIC changes include any steps done to alter
the PIXELS in the image so that it is different from the ones original recorded.

But before you do anything,

MAKE A COPY OF THE IMAGE FILE ! !

The best thing about EDITING is the **UNDO** option. Find it in the program right away, and use it to reverse the 'last' thing you did (some programs allow multiple steps backward). Anything you try can be reversed with UNDO.

The most common FORMAT changes include the following.

» RED EYE reduction removes (or blacks out) the reflection of the flash off an eye's retina. I prefer RED EYE EDIT to using the RED EYE FLASH setting which I find causes people to think the picture is over before it is (there are two flashes). A better trick is to ask all subjects to look at your shoulder (if you are holding the camera) rather than at the lens or your face. This causes the pupil to shift down just enough to avoid reflection.

» CROP allows you to choose a new rectangle from anywhere on the picture. This is a fun tool to get unique angles (the cat in the previous section was not cropped, he simply was looking at himself in the lens). CROP is also helpful if you have left too much FRAME in the shot.

» ROTATE turns it from landscape (horizontal) to portrait (vertical). This is great if you have not turned on the adjustment for the camera to do so. Be cautious in both instances because 'automatic' cropping can occur that significantly changes the image (and it can't be undone).

» FILTERS (not a lens you add, but the software kind) change the image appearance but I include them here because they can be reversed. Here you can change the picture to black and white, sepia, and more.

» BRIGHTNESS, which often has CONTRAST with it, is great for adding light to an image to bring out detail. Again, always take a picture too dark rather than too light (dark has details that a bright image doesn't).

Unless you love spending time trying to alter images, the **FORMAT** changes may be all you want to know. I suggest, however, that you continue reading, because every once in a while you will have an image that you feel would be just **perfect** if only. . . and at that point, you might want to know about some of the **ARTISTIC** editing tools that can turn an 'almost' perfect picture to a really impressive shot.

But in order to work on an image copy (never the original), there must be understanding that

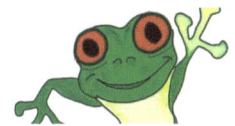 art is really made, in

LAYERS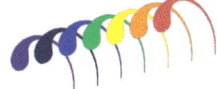

because, even after years of working in them, I get tripped up by layers more than any other aspect of software. The concept itself is pretty simple: instead of 'working on' or 'altering' the image file directly, you may work on a copy of it (sitting on top of it) that is transparent. And any additions to the image (text or more pieces of other pictures) usually become another layer (think overhead transparency on top of previous layer). Making sure you create a layer when you need to, and being sure you are working on the layer you really mean to, takes practice and patience. So always start by saving a copy of the image (you can use the duplicate feature as long as you duplicate the **FILE** not the **LAYER**).

And then, I always do duplicate the **LAYER** as well in my new copy because some **TOOLS** don't work on the **BACKGROUND LAYER**. For clarity, I then 'turn off' viewing of the background layer (in the best programs there is an eye that you click on or off), but I don't delete it.

The one FORMAT change that is critical for all of us is

image size

because our friends and family don't like waiting forever to open a 5 MP picture in an e-mail. Again, do NOT change the original image file, WORK ON A COPY! Simply choose the option to RESIZE and follow the prompts of your program to do it. The software will 'RESAMPLE' the pixels and compute the best image at a smaller file size, suitable for web display. There is a disadvantage to sending a smaller file size; you CAN'T PRINT IT LARGE without it PIXELATING. So I send small files with a note to that effect and offer to send the big file if they want to print (or I upload to a print-site and give them printing privileges). This brings up another point about image size and quality which is why a picture looks so good on you computer and not as good when printed. First, though the computer screen is only 72 DPI (dots per inch), there is light behind each dot (making it brighter). Second, printers all translate the RGB of the camera into CMYK in their own way which can change color quality. Additionally, if you print at anything less than 230 DPI (and printers use a different measure than DPI), the resulting picture just won't look good. Best is 300 DPI.

So re-size an image to send it out by e-mail, or to print standard 4x6 at home (re-sized can save printer ink without apparent loss of image quality).

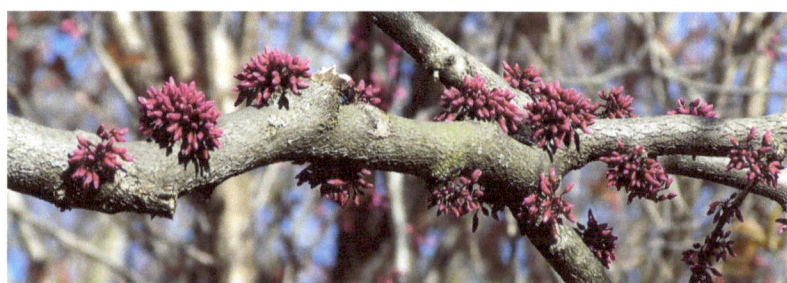

There are more ARTISTIC tools in most software than I can cover in this book, but I think a short review of some of the best TOOLS and TECHNIQUES will get your interest and give you some editing ideas.

» SELECTION TOOLS are how you 'choose' a portion of the image. The LASSO is how you choose a FREEFORM shape. The RECTANGLE (or MARQUEE) chooses a rectangle. If you have a newer program, there might be a tool that allows you to select similar PIXELS (fun for changing colors).

» HEALING TOOLS come in various styles to do retouching of flaws in the images (like glare or spots of lighter color).

» CLONE STAMP TOOLS come in various sizes to copy pixels from one area of an image to another. While this tool takes some practice (you pick a starting point by placing it there and using whatever KEY-SET your program calls for, and then place it in the new location where you want to 'overwrite' pixels); the trick is that however you move the arrow at the new location, the PIXELS from the old location replicate in tandem. You have to watch what you are doing and re-start as needed. This tool is worth trying because you can 'airbrush' out figure flaws and all other manner of problems with perfectly matched colors.

» ERASER TOOLS come in different sizes and degrees of opacity. Be cautious with an eraser because what is under it is nothing but the paper you print on.

» GRADIENT TOOLS can make the image transparent; uniformly or on a line (like the image behind this text).

» **EYEDROPPER TOOL** is one way to fill in the white spaces you get from an **ERASER** tool. You choose the **EYEDROPPER** and then click it on the color in your image that you want to match. The software creates the exact (but not always perfect) match to the 'spot that you touched.' Some of the time, that spot isn't the color your perfect brain thought it was getting so you have to try again, slightly moving the eyedropper. Keep in mind, the **EYEDROPPER** simply sets the color, it doesn't put it anywhere! ! ! A lot of new users get frustrated because they think it will **DROP** color once you pick it. Not so. Now you must go to an appropriate 'color- adding' tool like a **PENCIL, BRUSH, BUCKET,** or whatever.

» **TEXT TOOL** is the best holiday card tool ever. Use it to type a greeting that becomes part of the image. Choose the font (style of type) that you like and the size (usually expressed as **pt** or point, where **12 pt** is what you are reading here, and it can go up or down from there). Remember, when working with type, that screen view is not the same as print view. If your software allows it, use the capability to see print view before you print!

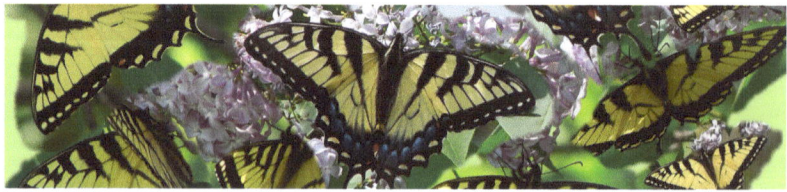

Have fun with your images by always working on a copy. Take the time to play with your editing software to see what you can do. You can simply improve the image you have, or turn it into something completely new. You can create collages of lots of pictures (we do that for holidays, and trips, and events, and subjects). Take the time to play first, because then you won't get frustrated when you really need to edit.

FINALLY

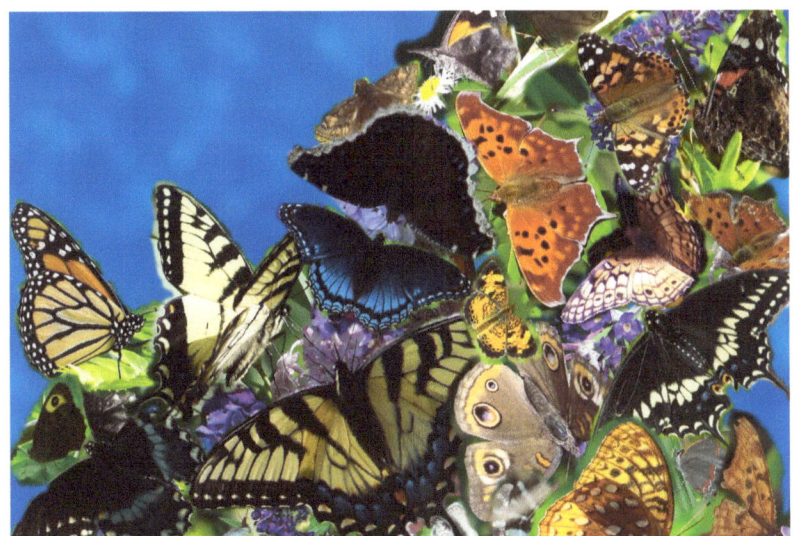

There is so much you can learn about photography with a digital camera because it is a very forgiving tool, unlike film photography, where every image costs to take it, to process it, and to print it. With the digital world, you can take thousands of images, keep hundreds and never print a one. Sure the camera costs, and the computer or digital display unit costs, but these are like having an entire photo processing center (which only the very advantaged were able to do with film).

DEMYSTIFYING DIGITAL PHOTOGRAPHY covers what an everyday photographer needs to know about the camera, the printing, the editing and computers. It gives you a framework for understanding the "method and magic" of the software in the camera and how it is meant to process light, because that is all that we are doing, capturing light for later viewing; light writing as the Greeks would say.

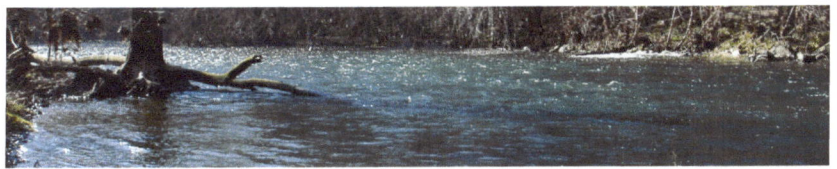

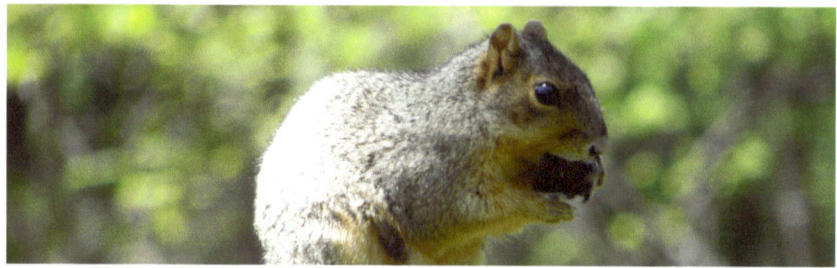

I am going to share a few final hints, tips, and ideas that will encourage you in your exploration of your camera, the images it helps you capture, and ways to do some new and interesting things.

• PORTRAITS can be a difficult to do. I think it is easier if you go to them and have them do something they love.
» to limit a double chin, have them sigh, then touch the tip of their tongue to the roof of their mouth while gently smiling
» edit the image to a 'softer' more forgiving look by keeping the background layer at 100% opacity and placing an exact copy on top of it as another layer at 70% opacity (or more or less, to get the 'feel' you desire)
» use a mirror to take a picture of the person's reflection over their shoulder (no flash!) so that you see their back and their reflection in frame; or use an acrylic mirror and flashlight to 'spotlight' the person (you may need an assistant, or at least a tripod and timer, for this one)

• FILTERS are pretty much a 35 mm camera thing ***except*** for a UV filter which will limit 'bouncing' light

• CHECK THE FRAME on your viewfinder by using a rectangle of colored paper that is a ratio of 2 by 3 (what most images print at). Take a photo of the rectangle centered in your LCD and/or viewfinder, and then check it on the computer and at the printer that you normally use to print. Practice getting it centered and 'all-in' frame.

- **NEVER SHOOT WITH LIGHT BEHIND YOUR SUBJECT** without taking steps to compensate for 1) the shadows it will cause, and 2) the way the camera will 'read' the scene. Force or **FILL FLASH** can help, but if your camera has a **SCENE SETTING** that addresses this situation, use it!

- **ORGANIZE** your pictures on a regular basis. Review them in the camera (delete true junk); upload them, review and delete more. Tag them so you can find them later.

- **ALWAYS PRINT** any picture you really care about. The digital camera only became affordable for most of us in the last decade, and the technology is changing fast (just like the home movie). The medium of storage might change and your computer might crash (even if you have a back-up). Without a print, you have lost access.

- **COPYRIGHT** and **PROPERTY RIGHT** rules apply to everything you shoot. Do some research, but in general, **RESPECT** other people's land, art, and images. Get permission (signed if you plan to use the image anywhere) for the person, the property, and the art. You cannot profit from something someone else owns.

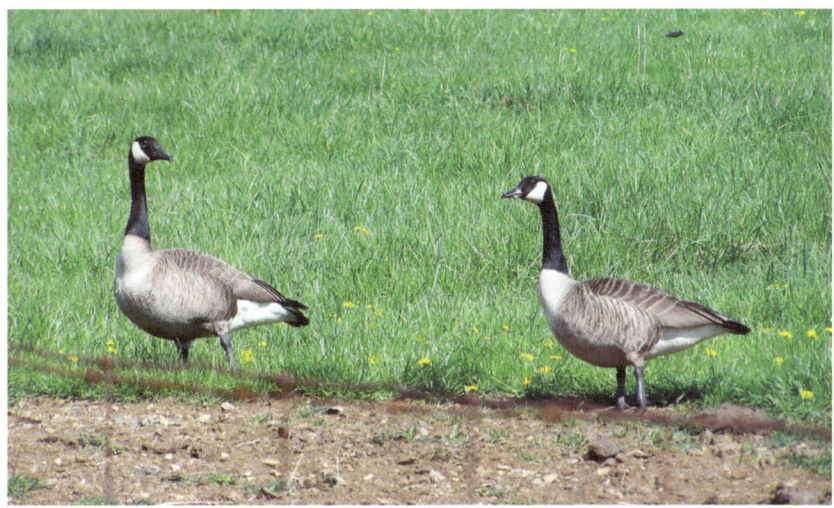

And finally, I encourage you wholeheartedly to

use your pictures

as cards, as gifts, as entries into contests and art shows. Make a slideshow of them for family viewing at gatherings. Make slideshows of them for fun.

There are sites online where you can put them on shirts, buttons, sneakers, and skateboards. You can make books with just pictures, or you can add words (a lot or a few). I did this book on my own, but I will send its files to a print on demand site so that people everywhere can learn.

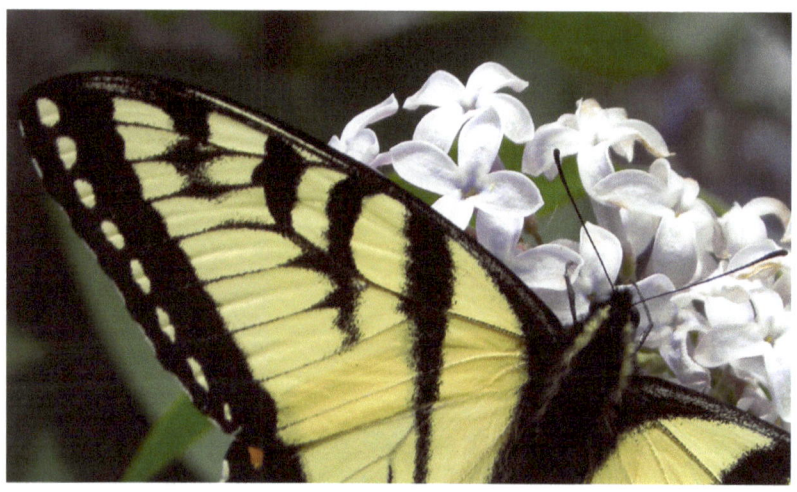

But most of all,

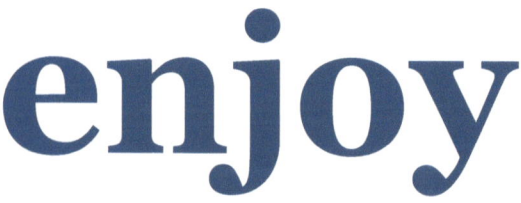

ABOUT

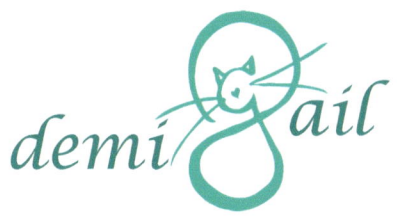

It is surprising to me, but I have been taking pictures for a lifetime. I babysat before I was 12 and bought an instamatic camera with my earnings. I posed my whole class in eighth grade and still have many of those pictures. I took pictures for my college newspaper, did interviews and photographs of scientists, and studied both film and photography in support of my writing degree. I have taken week by week pictures of my children in their first year. I have had many cameras, did film processing in my parents 'back bathroom' (the one without a window). I love doing close up pictures of butterflies and other small creatures. I do great portraits as gifts. But most of all, I love sharing the wonder of taking good pictures with anyone, anytime, anywhere. In a brief encounter in a receiving line (wedding one time, funeral another) I can, and have, solved 'issues' that got in the way of success for a would-be photographer.

I have loved distilling my class materials into this format so that more people can master the digital camera they already have and begin to enjoy the thrill of seeing their vision captured by what they do.

My work is online at www.demigail.com. There you will find access to some of the sites that I like for turning pictures into projects. You can also get my e-dress there. I always have time to hear what you have to say!

I prefer the self-portrait cartoon on the cover to photographs of myself, but I include this image of myself (taken by my agreeable husband) with a scene chosen for use in our new local hospital. I submitted many images to the hospital, but this one, taken with the same low cost camera as this shot of me, was chosen. It is a testament to the reality that

IT IS NOT THE CAMERA

that determines a 'winning' shot, but the

WILLINGNESS TO TAKE THE SHOT

with whatever you've got. I took the picture of the fall fog on my way home from an 'early' run to the High School with one of the children. On the way to, I saw the scene (but we were late). On the way back home, I stopped and shot six frames. It is as peaceful an image as it seems here and on the cover. So stop when you see a scene, and take that shot with the camera you've got.

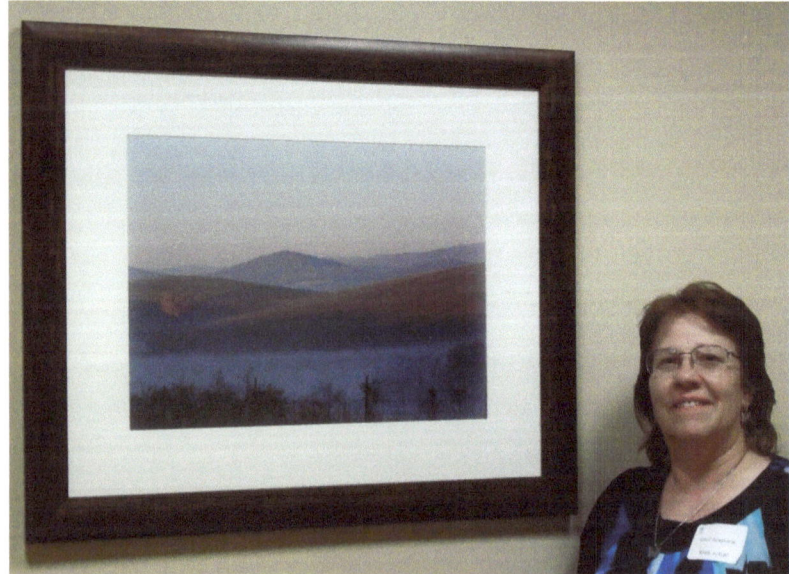